PRESIDENTS WHO DARED

Dwight D. Eisenhower

John F. Kennedy

Lyndon B. Johnson

EDMUND LINDOP

TWENTY-FIRST CENTURY BOOKS
A Division of Henry Holt and Company
New York

Twenty-First Century Books
A Division of Henry Holt and Company, Inc.
115 West 18th Street
New York, NY 10011

Henry Holt® and colophon are trademarks of
Henry Holt and Company, Inc.
Publishers since 1866

Published in Canada by Fitzhenry & Whiteside Ltd.
195 Allstate Parkway, Markham, Ontario L3R 4T8

Library of Congress Cataloging-in-Publication Data
Dwight D. Eisenhower, John F. Kennedy, Lyndon B. Johnson /
Edmund Lindop. — 1st ed.
p. cm. — (Presidents who dared)
Includes bibliographical references and index.
1. Presidents—United States—Biography—Juvenile literature. 2. Eisenhower,
Dwight D. (Dwight David), 1890–1969—Juvenile literature. 3. Kennedy, John F.
(John Fitzgerald), 1917–1963—Juvenile literature. 4. Johnson, Lyndon B.
(Lyndon Baines), 1908–1973—Juvenile literature. 5. United States—Politics and
government—1953–1961—Juvenile literature. 6. United States—Politics and gov-
ernment—1961–1963—Juvenile literature. 7. United States—Politics and government—1963–1969—Juvenile literature. I. Title. II. Series.
E176.1.L525 1996
973.92'092'2—dc20   95–40736
[B]   CIP
                                                            AC

ISBN 0–8050–3404–8
First Edition 1996

Printed in the United States of America
All first editions are printed on acid-free paper ∞.
10 9 8 7 6 5 4 3 2 1

Cover design by Robin Hoffman
Interior design by Kelly Soong

Photo credits
Copyright by White House Historical Association,
photographs by National Geographic Society:
Cover (left) and p. 8: *Dwight D. Eisenhower* by J. Anthony Wills
Cover (right) and p. 40: *Lyndon B. Johnson* by Elizabeth Shoumatoff

Courtesy of Bachrach, Inc.:
Cover (center) and p. 22

For Ryan, Kayla, and Megan Ostiller

CONTENTS

This book discusses Dwight D. Eisenhower, the thirty-fourth president; John F. Kennedy, the thirty-fifth president; and Lyndon B. Johnson, the thirty-sixth president.

Dwight D. Eisenhower was a military hero before he became president in 1953. During World War II, he commanded the Allied forces that defeated Adolf Hitler's powerful war machine in North Africa and in Western Europe. As the first Republican president in twenty years, Eisenhower dared to follow a moderate course, generally cooperating with a Congress controlled by the Democrats.

When Democrat John F. Kennedy moved into the White House in 1961, he had to deal with the Cold War between Communist and democratic nations. In the most dangerous crisis, he dared to send American ships to blockade Communist Cuba, preventing Soviet vessels carrying nuclear missiles from reaching that island.

After the assassination of Kennedy in November 1963, Lyndon B. Johnson became president. He dared to champion the most far-reaching civil rights laws in American history and to promote a bold program of economic and social reforms. Johnson's domestic achievements, however, were overshadowed by his decision to greatly expand the U.S. role in the tragic Vietnam War.

1

DWIGHT D. EISENHOWER

"I Like Ike" became one of the most famous slogans in American history. "Ike" was the nickname of Dwight D. Eisenhower, who—first as a general and later as a president—gained the respect and affection of millions of people throughout the world.

There was nothing in Ike's childhood to suggest that he would become a towering figure on the world stage. He was born on October 14, 1890, in a rented room near the railroad tracks in Denison, Texas. The next year his family moved to Abilene, Kansas. His father found a job there as a mechanic in the local creamery, where butter and cheese were made.

One of six boys in a hardworking, deeply religious family, Ike learned to do many chores. He and his brothers tended the garden and sold some of the vegetables to earn a little money for the family. The brothers took turns shoveling coal, raking leaves, and helping their mother clean the house, do the laundry, and cook the meals. The Eisenhowers were a closely knit, loving family, and every night the parents and children each read a passage from the Bible aloud.

"I have found out in later years we were very poor," Ike said in 1952, when the cornerstone of the Eisenhower Museum was laid in Abilene, across the street from his boyhood home. "But the glory of America is that we didn't know it then. All that we knew was that our parents—of great courage—could say to us, 'Opportunity is all about you. Reach out and take it.'"[1]

Like other families, the Eisenhowers occasionally had quarrels among themselves. Once Ike's parents would not let him go out with his two older brothers for Halloween trick or treating because they felt he was too young and might be harmed by the town bullies. This made Ike so mad that he rushed outside and pounded his fists against the trunk of a tree, hitting it again and again until he tore the skin from his fingers and they bled badly. When he finally went to bed sobbing, his mother put salve on his fingers and bandaged the worst cuts. She gently explained to her unhappy son that when he expressed anger and hatred, no one was injured but himself. Many years later, Ike recalled that his mother's advice provided "one of the most valuable moments of my life. To this day," he said, "I make it a practice to avoid hating anyone."[2]

Young Ike's favorite sports were football and baseball, and he played both these games on the Abilene High School teams. But while he was a student, the school had no coaches or money for athletic equipment, uniforms, or transportation to and from games. The players themselves had to raise the necessary funds. They collected enough money to pay for their equipment and uniforms but had nothing left for traveling expenses.

When the football team was scheduled to play Chapman High School, twelve miles away, there was no money to buy train tickets. Ike wrestled with this problem and finally came up with an idea. "We'll hop a freight train," he said. "If we're all on the same train, we'll outnumber the brakemen. Even if they see us they won't dare to shove us all off."[3] The team followed Ike's suggestion. They all boarded a freight train headed to Chapman, defeated their opponents on the football field, and then joyfully rode the rails home.

After graduating from high school in 1909, Ike worked more than a year at various jobs, earning money to help his brother Edgar pay his expenses at the University of Michigan. Then, attracted by the opportunity for a free college education, Ike applied to become a student at the U.S. Naval Academy at Annapolis, Maryland. He was deeply disappointed to learn that, at the age of twenty, he was already too old to be admitted to the academy. But in 1911, he was accepted for admission to the U.S. Military Academy at West Point, New York.

Ike was above-average in his college studies, but his strongest interest was to play on the Army football team. During his freshman year he ate large meals, increasing his weight from about 155 pounds to 175 pounds. His weight was nearly all solid muscle, evenly distributed along his sturdy five feet ten inches.

In his sophomore year, Ike made the varsity team as a hard-driving halfback. Sportswriters were impressed by his speed and strength, and some of them began calling him the "Kansas Cyclone." A *New York Times* reporter praised the future president as "one of the most promising backs in Eastern football."[4]

Then, in the next to last game of the season, Ike wrenched his knee, severely tearing the cartilage and tendons. A short time later he was taking part in a regular horseback riding drill, and when he jumped to the ground he hurt the same knee again. A doctor examined him and told Ike that his football-playing days were over. The young cadet was very disappointed at first, but his spirits improved when the athletic department let him help coach the Army freshman team.

When Eisenhower graduated from West Point in 1915 as a second lieutenant, he was assigned to the Nineteenth Infantry at Fort Sam Houston, Texas. One Sunday afternoon, as he was starting to make an inspection of guard posts, Ike noticed a small group of people across the street. Lulu Harris, the wife of a major, was in the group. "Ike," she called, "won't you come over here? I have some people I'd like you to meet."

"Sorry, Mrs. Harris," he replied. "I'm on guard and have to start an inspection trip."

"We didn't ask you to come over to stay. Just come over here and meet these friends of mine," she insisted.

The young lieutenant was then introduced to John Doud, a prosperous businessman from Denver, Colorado, and his family. "The one who attracted my eye instantly," wrote Eisenhower in his memoirs, "was a vivacious and attractive girl, smaller than average, saucy in the look about her face and in her whole attitude."[5]

This nineteen-year-old woman was Mamie Geneva Doud. She and Ike dated for several months and were married in July 1916. They had two sons, Doud Dwight, who died of scarlet fever at the age of three, and John, who followed in his father's footsteps by attending West Point and serving in the U.S. Army for many years.

During his long military career, Ike was stationed at many posts and performed a variety of military duties. When the United States entered World War I in 1917, he wanted to be sent overseas to fight in France. Instead, he was kept in the United States as an instructor at various military camps. The war ended one day before he was scheduled to sail to France.

After the war, Eisenhower served in the Panama Canal Zone for two years and then at bases in the United States. He rose in rank, first to captain and then to major. In 1926, he was sent to the Army General Staff School at Fort Leavenworth in Kansas and later to the Army War College, where he learned how to command large numbers of troops. His administrative abilities earned him a high position on the staff of the assistant secretary of war from 1929 to 1932.

In 1932, Eisenhower was appointed aide to General Douglas MacArthur, at that time chief of staff of the U.S. Army. When General MacArthur was sent as military adviser to the Philippines in 1935, Ike went along as his assistant. During the four years he spent on the islands, Ike became a lieutenant colonel, learned to fly, and helped train Filipino soldiers and pilots.

When Eisenhower returned to the United States in 1940, there were fewer than fifty thousand soldiers in the U.S. Army. Yet at that time World War II had already begun, and the Nazi forces of German dictator Adolf Hitler were quickly conquering one European country after another. Ike had to assume important tasks in helping rearm the United States—as quickly as possible! In the spring of 1941, Colonel Eisenhower became chief of staff of the Third Army that was training in Texas. That summer, he commanded large maneuvers held in Louisiana by the Second and Third Armies and won promotion to brigadier general.

After the Japanese attacked Pearl Harbor on

December 7, 1941, the United States entered the war against the Axis powers—Japan, Germany, Italy, and a few other countries. One week later, Eisenhower was summoned to Washington by the U.S. Army Chief of Staff General George C. Marshall. Ike was soon ordered to prepare detailed plans for a massive attack against German-held France, starting from a point across the English Channel in Great Britain.

Eisenhower worked hard on the plans for this important mission. When he completed them, General Marshall told him that "these are the orders you're to operate under. You're in command."[6] Ike was surprised and pleased to be appointed commander of the U.S. forces in Europe. But he knew that many months would pass before he could launch a successful invasion of Western Europe because Hitler's war machine was extremely powerful.

The general from Abilene, Kansas, had no training as a diplomat, but he showed great talent for combining officers and armies of different nations into a single team. He worked closely with the military leaders of the Allied nations of Great Britain and Canada. (The Soviet Union also was one of the Allies, but its forces were tied down in fighting valiantly against the huge German armies that had occupied large parts of its land.)

The Allies decided to strike first at Hitler's troops that had captured French colonies and were threatening Egypt in North Africa. Eisenhower commanded the Allied invasions of North Africa in November 1942. After this victorious campaign, the Allies mounted successful assaults against Sicily and Italy in 1943. Meanwhile, in February 1943, Ike was appointed to the rank of a four-star general.

In June 1944, the Allies finally were strong enough to

attempt the world's largest amphibious invasion—to cross the English Channel and attack the Germans at several beaches along the coast of the French province of Normandy. As supreme commander of the Allied Expeditionary Forces in Europe, Eisenhower assembled for the invasion more than 155,000 troops, more than 5,000 ships and boats, and 12,000 aircraft. This crucial mission, called Operation Overlord, would play a major role in determining the outcome of the war. "We cannot afford to fail," Eisenhower said grimly.[7]

The day originally set for the invasion was June 5, 1944, but stormy weather forced a postponement. The attackers needed a low tide at dawn to make beaches accessible and a full moon at night to provide light for paratroopers. Weather experts believed there might be a short break in the storm on June 6, but they could not predict just how long it would last. They felt the right combination of a low tide at dawn would not come again until June 19.

"The question is," wondered Eisenhower, "how long you can hang this operation on the end of a limb? . . . I am quite positive we must give the order. . . . O.K. Let's go!"[8] With his approval, the awesome attack across the English Channel began on June 6, which came to be known as "D Day."

Millions of people throughout the free world tensely waited to learn whether the Allies would gain footholds on the beaches of Normandy or be driven back into the sea. The fighting was savage, the casualties were heavy on both sides, but the invasion forces were successful. The German troops were forced to retreat, first from Normandy, then from large areas of France and Belgium, and finally, over the next eight months, into Germany itself. The Nazis, who also were being driven back on the eastern front by the Soviets, surrendered in May 1945. The war in Europe was finally over, but fighting against Japan continued until after the Americans dropped atomic bombs on Hiroshima and Nagasaki in August.

Eisenhower returned to the United States a towering hero. Greeted by huge, cheering throngs in one city after another, he stood in the back of an open car, waving his arms and flashing a broad, familiar grin to the enthusiastic crowds. He was so popular that leaders of both the Democratic and Republican Parties urged him to run for the presidency in 1948, but Ike declined their offers.

For a short time he served as president of Columbia University in New York City. Then in 1951, as the Cold War between the Communist Soviet Union and the democratic nations grew more intense, Eisenhower was called back to military duty. He served as commander of the North Atlantic Treaty Organization (NATO) forces that were being assembled for the common defense of North America and its European allies. During the next eighteen months, he organized the various NATO armed services into a strong, unified combat group.

The pressure on Eisenhower to run for the presidency continued to mount, and finally in 1952 he agreed to seek the nomination. To become the Republican candidate he first had to defeat Senator Robert A. Taft of Ohio, a highly respected leader of the party. At the national convention, a large number of delegates displayed signs saying "I Like Ike" and "We Like Ike." Eisenhower won the nomination, and the Republicans selected Senator Richard M. Nixon of California as his vice presidential running mate.

Ike's Democratic opponent was Governor Adlai E.

Stevenson of Illinois. He gave eloquent speeches, but a large number of voters believed that the homespun general who had achieved victory on the battlefield would become an outstanding president. Winning 55 percent of the popular vote, Eisenhower easily defeated Stevenson.

During the presidential campaign, the Korean War was one issue that greatly concerned the American public. It had started in 1950 when Communist North Korea invaded South Korea. The United Nations, led by forces from the United States, had come to the defense of South Korea. But the war dragged on, and when candidate Eisenhower dramatically pledged in 1952, "I shall go to Korea" to try to find a solution to the stalemated conflict, many Americans cheered. President-elect Eisenhower kept his promise, and before his inauguration made a trip to Korea. The war did not end immediately, but about six months later a peace treaty was signed.

Eisenhower, the first Republican president in twenty years, worked more closely with Congress than did most of the presidents who followed him into the White House. In his first year in office, 89.2 percent of the bills that he asked for were passed by Congress: none of the next eight presidents had as high a rate of success for their legislative agenda in their first year of office. As a result of the 1954 congressional elections, the Democrats gained control of both houses of Congress. But Ike continued to cooperate with Congress, and this provided important new laws.

In domestic affairs, President Eisenhower launched a middle-of-the-road policy that he called "dynamic conservatism." He tried to abolish or at least decrease the scope of many activities previously carried out by the federal government. He ordered government spending reduced and eliminated the jobs of 183,000 federal employees. The president also signed into law measures that lowered taxes.

One controversial issue during the Eisenhower administration was whether the national government or the states should control the oil fields that were located in the water near the coasts of various states. The president, who was eager to curb some of the powers of the federal government, supported the transfer of control over these offshore oil fields to the states, and Congress approved this measure in 1953.

On the other hand, Ike accepted and even advanced some programs established under President Franklin D. Roosevelt's New Deal. Social Security benefits were extended, and the minimum wage was raised to $1 an hour. In a public works project that dwarfed anything the New Deal had attempted, Eisenhower supported a $27 billion program to build 42,000 miles of fast interstate highways, linking all parts of the nation. Construction of many of the freeways that we use today was begun at that time.

The Cold War between Communist and non-Communist countries grew more dangerous in the 1950s when both the United States and the Soviet Union developed the hydrogen bomb—a nuclear device hundreds of times more powerful than the atomic bomb. President Eisenhower worked to strengthen the defense of the United States, approving the construction of intercontinental ballistic missiles and nuclear-powered submarines. At the same time, he worked hard to advance the cause of world peace. "War," the former general wrote, "is the most stupid and tragic of human ventures."[9]

In 1953, he proposed an "atoms-for-peace" plan in which all nations would pool their atomic materials and knowledge for the benefit of humankind. Even though the Soviets did not support this plan, the International Atomic Energy Agency was created. But the agency lacked the power to prevent the spread of nuclear weapons.

The United States faced a major decision involving Indochina in 1954. The Communist natives were fighting to free this Asian colony from the control of France. Vice President Nixon and Secretary of State John Foster Dulles urged Eisenhower to send military forces to help the French. But he refused to involve the United States in a war without the support of other countries or Congress. (The French were defeated, and Indochina later was divided into Laos, Cambodia, and South and North Vietnam.)

The American president went to a summit meeting in 1955 at Geneva, Switzerland. There he talked with Nikita Khrushchev, the head of the Soviet government, and the leaders of Great Britain and France. Eisenhower dramatically called for an "open skies" policy, by which the four big world powers would allow one another to make aerial inspections and take photographs of their military sites. Khrushchev, however, turned down this proposal.

Later that year, while on a golfing vacation in Colorado, Ike suffered a serious heart attack. He remained in the hospital for seven weeks. In mid-November he was well enough to fly back to Washington and then travel to Gettysburg, Pennsylvania, where he and Mamie owned a farm with a comfortable house.

The president completely recovered from his heart attack, but many people wondered if he would run at the age of sixty-six for a second term in the White House. He had already spent more than forty years in the service of his country, but many problems still needed to be solved.

So, on February 29, 1956, he said at a press conference, "I have reached a decision. My answer will be positive."[10] Ike agreed to run for another term as president.

His second-term opponent again was Democrat Adlai E. Stevenson. In this 1956 rematch, Ike won by an even larger margin than in his first race against Stevenson.

At Eisenhower's request, in 1957 Congress passed the first major civil rights legislation since 1875. It provided penalties for violation of the voting rights of blacks and all other American citizens. An even stronger civil rights bill was enacted in 1960.

In 1957, Governor Orval Faubus of Arkansas called out the state's National Guard to prevent the court-ordered enrollment of black students at Central High School in Little Rock. When the Arkansas governor refused to withdraw the National Guard, President Eisenhower sent U.S. Army troops to Little Rock. These soldiers then escorted the black students to their classes.

During the Eisenhower administration, the Middle East was one of the most unstable areas in the world. In addition to the extreme tension between the Israelis and their Arab neighbors, there was the constant fear of Communist takeovers in that region. So in 1957, President Eisenhower obtained approval from Congress to use American military forces to defend any country in the Middle East that was threatened by Communist aggression. When the government of Lebanon requested such assistance in 1958, Eisenhower sent U.S. Marines to protect that tiny Middle Eastern country.

One of Eisenhower's proudest accomplishments was the joint construction by the United States and Canada of the St. Lawrence Seaway, a waterway linking the Atlantic

Ocean and the Great Lakes. The seaway made it possible for large ocean-going ships to sail into the Great Lakes and trade directly with the American Midwest. Work began on the system's canals and locks in 1954, and the seaway was opened by President Eisenhower and British Queen Elizabeth II in 1959.

Eisenhower planned to attend another summit meeting in which he could again talk with Soviet Premier Khrushchev about easing the tensions of the Cold War. But shortly before the scheduled meeting in Paris in May 1960, the Soviets shot down an American U-2 high-altitude spy plane flying over Soviet territory and captured its pilot. Eisenhower admitted that spy flights over Russia had been going on but defended them as necessary for national security. Enraged, Khrushchev called off the meeting.

Before he stepped down from the presidency, Eisenhower addressed the nation on television in January 1961. He warned his audience not to bow to the "recurring temptations" that military action is "the miraculous solution to all current difficulties" in foreign affairs. He said that Americans must guard against the pressures of vast powers "new in American experience—the immense military establishment and a large arms industry."[11]

Eisenhower retired to his Gettysburg farm, where he wrote his memoirs and golfed regularly. At the age of seventy-eight, he died on March 28, 1969, and was buried in Abilene, Kansas.

Lyndon B. Johnson, who as Senate majority leader had worked closely with President Eisenhower, said of him: "The sturdy and enduring values—honor, courage, integrity, decency—all found eloquent expression in the life of this good man and noble leader."[12]

2

JOHN F. KENNEDY

When Dwight D. Eisenhower stepped down from the presidency in 1961 at the age of seventy, he was followed into the White House by a man young enough to be his son. Forty-three-year-old John Fitzgerald Kennedy became the youngest American ever elected president. He also was the first president born in the twentieth century.

The Kennedy family had a long tradition of being deeply involved in politics. John's paternal grandfather served in both houses of the Massachusetts legislature. John's mother, Rose Fitzgerald Kennedy, was the daughter of an even more prominent politician, who held offices in the Massachusetts Senate and the U.S. House of Representatives before serving for six years as mayor of Boston.

Born in Brookline, Massachusetts, on May 29, 1917, John Kennedy (who was usually called "Jack") grew up in a wealthy family. His father, Joseph P. Kennedy, acquired a fortune by shrewdly trading in stocks, producing movies, and making profitable real estate deals.

Jack had five sisters and three brothers. His sisters, all younger than Jack, were Rosemary, Kathleen, Eunice, Patricia, and Jean. He had one older brother, Joe Jr., and two younger brothers, Robert "Bobby" and Edward "Ted." Both Robert and Edward became United States senators.

When Jack was ten, his family moved to a suburb of

New York City, and he attended a nearby private school. A short time later the Kennedys bought a white clapboard ten-bedroom house on an estate in Hyannis Port, on Cape Cod, Massachusetts. The estate had more than two acres of land, tennis courts, and a private beach overlooking Nantucket Sound. It was here that Jack enjoyed playing tennis and football, became a strong swimmer, and learned how to sail boats expertly.

The Kennedy children entered many swimming meets and sailboat races. Their father was very competitive and expected his children to finish first in all sporting contests. "The thing he kept telling us," said Jack's sister Eunice, "was that coming in second was just no good. The important thing was to win."[1]

This pressure to win had both bad and good effects on Jack. It caused him to feel ashamed when he did not bring home a first-place medal from athletic contests. On the other hand, it helped him acquire the driving determination that later enabled him to survive life-threatening physical crises and to win political elections.

When Jack was fourteen, he enrolled at Choate, a highly ranked preparatory school in Wallingford, Connecticut. He soon discovered that his teachers expected him to follow closely in the footsteps of his brother Joe, who had won honors at Choate in both scholarship and sports. Jack, however, was not as good a student or athlete as his older brother.

He did not work hard at his studies and earned only average grades. But even though he was thin and not very fast, Jack was determined to succeed at playing football. "The most burning thing I can remember about Jack," said the Choate football coach, "was that he was a fighter. . . .

Joe, he was a real athlete. But Jack made up for what he lacked in athletic ability with his fight."[2]

Jack entered Harvard University in 1936, and again he had to compete with Joe's outstanding records. His confidence was shaken, and he felt ill at ease when he heard the professors praising his brother. They predicted that Joe would have a brilliant future, and his father urged Joe to pursue a career in politics.

While Jack performed on the Harvard swimming team, his chief athletic goal was to play on the college's football team. Six feet tall but a slim 150 pounds, he practiced diligently and made the most of his limited physical talents. In his sophomore year, through sheer persistence he won a position on the junior varsity squad. But scrimmaging one afternoon against the much heavier varsity team, Jack received a severe spinal injury from which he would suffer the rest of his life.

Joseph P. Kennedy was a friend of President Franklin D. Roosevelt and a large contributor to the Democratic Party. In 1937, President Roosevelt appointed Kennedy ambassador to Great Britain, and the large Kennedy clan moved to London. Jack visited his family during college vacations, and he spent the second semester of his junior year working as secretary to his father.

The Kennedys were in England during the time when Adolf Hitler, the ruthless dictator of Nazi Germany, was building a powerful war machine that easily gained control of helpless Austria and Czechoslovakia. Then, in September 1939, Nazi armed forces invaded Poland, which Britain and France had promised to protect. This act started World War II when Britain and France declared war against Germany.

Jack wanted to know why, in the late 1930s, England had appeased Hitler and failed to rearm to meet Germany's threat to world peace. He studied this subject thoroughly and then wrote about it in his senior thesis (research project) at Harvard. Later he polished his thesis, and in 1940 it was published as a book titled *Why England Slept*. The book became a best-seller in both the United States and England, and its twenty-three-year-old author donated his English book royalties to the bombed city of Plymouth, England.

In 1941, both Joe and Jack enlisted in the U.S. Naval Reserve, and they were called to active duty shortly after Japan attacked Pearl Harbor on December 7. At first Jack had a desk job, but he was eager to take part in the military action. Through his father's influence he was put in command of twelve men on a small, speedy patrol boat, PT-109, that sailed near the Solomon Islands in the South Pacific.

On the night of August 2, 1943, a Japanese destroyer smashed into PT-109, splitting the small patrol boat into two parts. Jack was hurled against the wall of the cockpit with such devastating force that the steering wheel was torn from his hands and his weak back was so severely reinjured that he felt it must have been broken. His first thought, he said afterward, was, "This is what it's like to be killed."[3]

Two members of the crew died instantly. The eleven other men survived, but several of them were badly burned because the stern, or back part of the boat, became engulfed in flames. The bow, or front section, was still afloat, and Lieutenant Kennedy ordered the sailors to huddle inside it until the night passed.

At daybreak the men began swimming toward an

island about three miles away. Despite the stabbing pain in his back, Jack not only managed to swim for more than three hours, but he also towed an injured companion by a life-jacket strap held in his teeth.

Several days later the stranded Americans were greeted on Olasana Island by two natives. Kennedy then used his knife to scratch a brief message for help on a coconut shell, and the natives delivered the coconut to a man in the Australian Navy. He got in touch with an American commander, and a PT boat was sent to pick up the shipwrecked sailors.

This incident earned Kennedy a Purple Heart, the Navy and Marine Corps Medal, and a citation from Admiral William Halsey for "extremely heroic conduct." But Jack was in constant pain from his back injury and was weakened by malaria, which caused him to lose twenty-five pounds. He had to leave the navy and was sent home to recuperate at a hospital in Massachusetts.

Tragedy struck the Kennedy family in August 1944. Joe, a navy pilot, was killed while flying a mission in Europe. In memory of his older brother, Jack asked his relatives and friends to write memorial essays that were included in a privately published book, *As We Remember Joe.*

Before Joe's death, Jack had not decided what he wanted to do with his life. He considered becoming a writer, a teacher, or a lawyer. But his father, who had expected his eldest son to go into public service, begged Jack to run for a political office.

At first Jack resisted this idea. Except when he was with his family or close friends, Jack was quite shy and reserved—not the outgoing, self-confident type of person that his older brother had been. His father, however, finally convinced Jack that since he now was the oldest Kennedy of his generation, he must carry on the family tradition and carve out a political career. "I'm it now, you know," he told a friend. "It's my turn. I've got to perform."[4]

Jack's first political target was a seat in the United States House of Representatives from a district located mainly in East Boston. Ten candidates ran for the 1946 Democratic nomination in this district, which was largely composed of blue-collar, working-class citizens. When they were introduced at political rallies, the other nine candidates often reminded voters that they had "come up the hard way" from families that were not wealthy. But when it was Jack's turn to take the microphone, he grinned and honestly admitted, "I'm the one who didn't come up the hard way."[5]

The Kennedy family plunged into Jack's political campaign. Jack's father made large financial contributions. His mother and sisters held luncheons and tea parties to attract women voters. Brother Bobby, only twenty years old, rang many doorbells and passed out thousands of campaign brochures. Jack shook hands with factory workers and store clerks from dawn to dusk. Addressing one rally after another, he gradually overcame his shyness and reached out to crowds through eloquent arguments sprinkled with Irish wit.

When the votes were counted, Kennedy had captured the Democratic primary by a two-to-one margin over his nearest opponent, and he easily defeated the Republican candidate in the general election. In 1948 and 1950 he was reelected to two more terms in the House of Representatives.

During his six years as a U.S. Representative from

Massachusetts, Kennedy compiled a moderately liberal voting record and served on the House Education and Labor Committee. He introduced a bill calling for federal funds for slum clearance and low-cost housing and lashed out at leaders of the American Legion who opposed the bill. Kennedy favored bills to extend Social Security benefits and to provide medical aid to the aged. He denounced the Taft-Hartley Act, which placed strict curbs on the activities of labor unions. In foreign affairs, he supported the Truman Doctrine to defend Greece and Turkey against Communist takeovers and the Marshall Plan to help Western European countries recover from the destruction caused by World War II.

In 1952, Jack ran for the Senate seat then held by Henry Cabot Lodge, a popular Republican. Following a strenuous campaign, Kennedy defeated Lodge by about 70,000 votes. This was a remarkable victory because, on the same day in the presidential race, Republican Dwight Eisenhower carried the state of Massachusetts by more than 200,000 votes. Kennedy was now hailed as one of the brightest young stars in the Democratic Party.

The previous year Jack had been introduced at a dinner party to Jacqueline "Jackie" Bouvier, a young woman of exceptional beauty and charm who belonged to a socially prominent family. Jackie was well educated, having studied at Vassar College and the Sorbonne in Paris before earning a degree from George Washington University in the nation's capital. She spoke French, Spanish, and Italian fluently. Following college she was hired by the *Washington Times-Herald* as an inquiring photographer, and in this job she interviewed and took pictures of many celebrities.

Jack was thirty-six years old and Jackie was twenty-four when they were married on September 12, 1953. Both were Catholic, and their wedding ceremony was performed by Archbishop Richard J. Cushing. At this spectacular social event there were thirteen bridesmaids, nine hundred guests, and several thousand gate-crashers, who nearly crushed the bride when they broke through ropes outside the church.

The Kennedys had three children. Caroline was born in 1957 and John Jr. three years later. Their third child, Patrick, was born with a breathing problem and lived less than two days.

Although Jack appeared strong and healthy in public, he had two serious ailments. He suffered from Addison's disease, a malfunction of the adrenal glands, and regularly took medicine to avoid its life-threatening complications. And his back hurt so much that he often had to walk with crutches. In 1954, he decided to undergo spinal fusion surgery in the hope it would relieve his back pain.

Several doctors opposed the delicate operation, fearing that his Addison's disease might trigger a fatal infection. Determined to take the risk, Jack pointed to his crutches and declared, "I'd rather be dead than spend the rest of my life on those things."[6]

The operation proved a failure, and when a dangerous infection developed, Jack slipped into a coma. For a time he seemed so close to death that he was given the last rites of the Catholic Church. Only after a few tense days did he open his eyes and begin to recover.

Four months later, he was strong enough to allow doctors to operate again. This operation was partially successful, but it did not end his back pain. During the long period in which he was recovering, Jack decided to write a book. With the help of his friend Ted Sorensen, Kennedy wrote about political figures in American history who had demonstrated unusual bravery. The book was called *Profiles in Courage*. It became a best-seller and won a Pulitzer Prize for biography.

At the 1956 Democratic National Convention, presidential nominee Adlai E. Stevenson told the delegates to select any vice presidential candidate they wanted. Before the first ballot, thirteen names, including Kennedy's, were placed in nomination. Kennedy briefly held the lead on the second ballot and came within forty votes of becoming Stevenson's running mate. But then enough delegates switched their votes to Senator Estes Kefauver of Tennessee to give him the nomination. In the general election, the Republican ticket of President Dwight D. Eisenhower and Vice President Richard Nixon easily defeated the Stevenson and Kefauver ticket. It was a stroke of good luck for Kennedy's political future that he had not been part of the Democrats' losing ticket.

Kennedy was reelected to the Senate in 1958 by the largest margin of votes ever given a candidate in Massachusetts at that time—a record 875,000 votes more than his Republican rival. Public opinion polls began showing him as the leading contender for the next presidential nomination by his party.

In 1960, Kennedy did enter the race for the presidential nomination of the Democratic Party. To mount a successful campaign, he knew he had to overcome certain handicaps—his family's wealth, his youth, and especially, his religion. No Catholic had ever won the presidency, and many voters in the largely Protestant United States feared that a Catholic president might come under the control of the Pope and other officials of the Catholic Church.

Campaigning in West Virginia, a state in which only 3 percent of the people were Catholics, Kennedy discussed the religious issue openly and forcefully. He emphasized that being a Catholic did not in any way affect his total commitment to the separation of church and state. He asked the voters to cast aside intolerance and bigotry. "For while this year it may be a Catholic against whom the finger of suspicion is pointed," he said, "in other years it has been, and may someday be again, a Jew—or a Quaker—or a Unitarian—or a Baptist. . . . Today I may be the victim—but tomorrow it may be you."[7]

Besides West Virginia, Kennedy entered presidential primary elections in six other states and won all of them. He also won the support of delegates in many states that did not have presidential primary elections, and the Democratic National Convention nominated him for the presidency. Then Kennedy asked Lyndon B. Johnson of Texas, the majority leader of the Senate, to be his running mate, and Johnson accepted the offer.

The Republicans selected Vice President Richard Nixon as their presidential nominee. Kennedy and Nixon were the first presidential candidates to debate on television. Millions of Americans were glued to their TV sets during the four debates. Both men performed well, but Kennedy appeared more poised, self-confident, and vigorous than his opponent. Many voters felt less concerned about Kennedy's youth after he responded maturely to the debate questions.

The election was the closest in the twentieth century. More than 68 million Americans went to the polls, and

Kennedy won the popular vote with 49.72 percent to Nixon's 49.55 percent. Kennedy received 303 electoral votes and Nixon 219, but if Nixon had carried Illinois and Texas—which he barely lost—he would have won the election.

On January 20, 1961, snow was falling and a bone-chilling wind swept through the Capitol steps where the nation's young new leader was sworn in as president. His short inaugural address is best remembered for this eloquent phrase that challenged his fellow Americans: "Ask not what your country can do for you; ask what you can do for your country."[8]

Some Americans responded to this challenge by enlisting in the Peace Corps, which Kennedy established shortly after he took office. This agency provided volunteers to teach and offer technical assistance to poor people in underdeveloped countries. About eighty-five thousand Americans, mostly young adults, served in the corps over the next twenty years.

Another Kennedy-sponsored program to raise the standard of living in impoverished countries also was launched in 1961. Called the Alliance for Progress, it pledged that the United States would provide billions of dollars in aid to Latin American nations to help them improve their economies and reduce the threat of takeover by Communist rulers.

Already one Communist dictator, Fidel Castro, had gained control of Cuba, a Caribbean island less than one hundred miles off the coast of Florida. While Eisenhower was still president, the U.S. Central Intelligence Agency (CIA) had developed a plan to overthrow Castro. It involved about fifteen hundred Cuban exiles who had fled their homeland and were eager to help end Castro's rule.

Trained secretly in Guatemala and outfitted with American weapons, the exiles' mission was to invade Cuba at Cochinos Bay (Bay of Pigs). Once they had established a beach-hold there, they believed the Cuban people would stage a revolt and topple Castro.

President Kennedy gave his consent for the mission to go ahead as planned. But when the armed exiles reached the Cuban shore in April 1961, they were met by an overwhelming force of Castro's soldiers and tanks. About eleven hundred of the invaders were taken prisoner, and the Cuban people did not revolt.

Some of the president's advisers then urged him to order American planes and ships to unleash a powerful attack on the small island nation. But Kennedy knew that direct interference by the United States in Cuban affairs would be strongly opposed by other Latin American countries and the Soviet Union, Cuba's close friend. So he refused to enlarge the military operation and accepted the blame for the mission's failure.

JFK (the first president since Franklin D. Roosevelt to be referred to by his initials) considered spaceflight as a major battleground in the Cold War between communism and the free world. Not only had the Soviets in 1957 sent up *Sputnik I*, the first artificial satellite to orbit the earth, but the powerful rockets that launched it meant that for the first time in its history the United States could be attacked by enemy weapons thousands of miles away. Then, in April 1961, Soviet astronaut Yuri Gagarin became the first person to orbit the earth in a spacecraft. When the president heard this startling news, he told a White House meeting that "there's nothing more important" than finding a way to catch up with the Soviets.[9]

A short time later, Kennedy appeared before Congress and requested huge funds in order to fulfill an astounding new mission in manned spaceflight. He said, "I believe this nation should commit itself to achieving the goal, before this decade is out, of landing a man on the moon and returning him safely to earth. No single space project in this period will be more impressive to mankind."[10] This heroic goal was reached in July 1969, during Nixon's administration, when astronauts Neil Armstrong and Edwin Aldrin walked on the moon and returned to the United States.

In the summer of 1961, President and Mrs. Kennedy traveled to Europe. Stopping first in France, Jackie captivated the diplomats in Paris with her glamorous appearance and her conversations in perfect French. Shortly before they departed for Vienna, Austria, JFK joked with reporters, saying, "I am the man who accompanied Jacqueline Kennedy to Paris."[11]

President Kennedy met Soviet Premier Nikita Khrushchev in Vienna. Khrushchev said he was planning to allow Communist East Germany to cut off all transportation routes to West Berlin, a free, democratic city that was located inside East Germany. Kennedy sternly replied that the United States would never abandon the people of West Berlin by permitting them to become isolated from the free world.

Khrushchev was angry because thousands of Germans were crossing from Communist East Berlin into non-Communist West Berlin. So in August 1961, the Communists built and patrolled a high wall in Berlin to prevent more East Berliners from escaping to freedom.

Later Kennedy visited the Berlin Wall, where he was

greeted by thousands of wildly cheering Germans. "All free men, wherever they may live," he told the crowd, "are citizens of Berlin, and therefore, as a free man, I take pride in the words: *Ich bin ein Berliner!*" ("I am a Berliner!")[12]

In October 1962, U.S. aerial photographs revealed that the Soviet Union was building nuclear missile bases in Cuba. Nuclear weapons launched from these bases would be capable of striking the eastern two-thirds of the United States. Alarmed by this frightening discovery, some of the president's advisers wanted U.S. planes to bomb the missile sites immediately. Other advisers suggested a naval blockade of the island to prevent the Soviets from shipping more nuclear war materials to Cuba. The blockade would be coupled with a demand that all Cuban missile sites be dismantled. JFK decided in favor of the blockade because it gave the Soviets the opportunity to back down without risking war with the United States.

American warships formed a chain across the Caribbean Sea five hundred miles from the Cuban coast. For several days, millions of Americans waited nervously as Soviet ships headed for Cuba moved across the Atlantic Ocean; never before had there been such a dangerous threat of a devastating nuclear war. But before the first Communist ships reached the American blockade, they turned around and sailed away. Premier Khrushchev then agreed to dismantle the Cuban missile sites and return the weapons to the Soviet Union in exchange for an American pledge not to invade Cuba.

Taking advantage of the Soviets' decision not to risk war with the United States, Kennedy urged that the two nations stop the dangerous tests of nuclear weapons in the atmosphere. After months of negotiations, in July 1963, the two superpowers—and eventually more than one hundred nations—approved the Nuclear Test Ban Treaty to end atmospheric tests of nuclear weapons. Although underground testing was still permitted, the ban on nuclear explosions in the skies sharply reduced the danger from radioactive fallout.

One of the most serious problems confronting the Kennedy administration was the need to extend to blacks and other minorities all of the civil rights enjoyed by other U.S. citizens. By executive orders, the president established the Committee on Equal Employment Opportunity and decreed the end of discrimination in housing owned, operated, or financed by the federal government. Also, federal troops were sent to assure the admission of black students to southern universities that previously had banned all African-Americans.

Violence broke out in April 1963 in Birmingham, Alabama, where civil rights supporters led by the Reverend Martin Luther King Jr. were peacefully marching to protest segregation in that city. The Birmingham police confronted the demonstrators with clubs, attack dogs, and high-pressure fire hoses. Televised pictures of this vicious conduct exposed to the nation the brutality of these white segregationists and led to angry demonstrations in many cities with large African-American populations.

President Kennedy addressed the nation on the civil rights issue in a televised broadcast on June 11, 1963. "Now the time has come for this nation to fulfill its promise," he said. "The events in Birmingham and elsewhere have so increased the cries for equality that no city or state or legislative body can prudently choose to ignore them. It is time to act in the Congress, in your state and local legislative body, and, above all, in all our daily lives."[13]

JFK then sent to Congress the most comprehensive civil rights bill in the nation's history. But some southern legislators believed that it called for too much change by overthrowing long-standing traditions, and they blocked passage of the bill.

President and Mrs. Kennedy visited Dallas, Texas, on November 22, 1963. They rode in the backseat of an open limousine behind Governor John B. Connally of Texas and his wife. A large, cheering crowd lined the streets of their motorcade, and Mrs. Connally turned to Kennedy and said, "You sure can't say Dallas doesn't love you, Mr. President."[14]

Suddenly shots rang out from the sixth floor of a warehouse called the Texas School Book Depository. The president, fatally shot through the head and throat, tumbled into his wife's lap. Governor Connally also was seriously wounded, but he later recovered. The limousine sped to a nearby hospital, where Kennedy was declared dead about half an hour after the shooting.

A short time later the police arrested Lee Harvey Oswald, an ex-marine and Communist sympathizer, who worked at the Texas School Book Depository. While fleeing the crime scene, he murdered a police officer who was trying to question him. Ballistic tests showed that Oswald owned the type of rifle that killed the president.

Oswald, however, was never brought to trial. While being transferred to a county jail, he was shot to death by Jack Ruby, a Dallas nightclub owner, who claimed that he was avenging the president's death.

The assassination of Kennedy was investigated by a

commission of government officials headed by Earl Warren, chief justice of the Supreme Court. After the commission talked to many witnesses and studied much evidence, it issued a report in 1964 that concluded that Oswald had killed the president and had acted alone.

In the years following Kennedy's death many people questioned the accuracy of the Warren Report. So Congress appointed a second commission in 1979 to delve again into the facts surrounding the assassination. The commission sought to discover whether Oswald had been ordered by some conspiracy to murder Kennedy, and if so, who the ringleaders of the conspiracy were. There also was a possibility that a second gunman shot at Kennedy from a grassy knoll across the street from the book depository.

When it completed its investigation, this second commission tended to support the idea that Oswald probably had not acted alone. But it failed to find definite information linking any other person or group to the tragic event. The full account of Kennedy's assassination remains shrouded in mystery.

The American public and free people everywhere grieved the loss of their youthful and vigorous leader. More perhaps as a shining beacon of inspiration than for his specific accomplishments, John F. Kennedy had provided a steadfast vision that all things are possible—from preventing nuclear warfare to reaching the moon.

The forty-six-year-old president was buried at Arlington National Cemetery near Washington, D.C. An eternal flame, lit by his wife, marks his grave. Every year hundreds of thousands of people pass by the fallen president's grave and pause at the flame burning in his honor.

3

LYNDON B. JOHNSON

"A United States senator was born today—my grandson!"[1] Sam Johnson Sr. rode his horse from farmhouse to farmhouse, happily proclaiming this exciting news to all who could hear his jubilant voice. Old Sam believed with all his heart that his grandson, Lyndon Baines Johnson, born on August 27, 1908, would become one of the nation's great political leaders.

To Sam's neighbors this seemed like a wild prediction, not to be taken seriously. Unlike the family of John F. Kennedy, the Johnsons could not boast of great wealth and political power. At the time of Lyndon's birth, his parents— Sam Johnson Jr. and Rebekah Baines Johnson—lived in a small farmhouse on the Pedernales River in central Texas. They had no electric lights or indoor toilets, and water had to be drawn from a pump outdoors.

Lyndon was the first of five children, and Sam Jr. had to struggle to support his family in the scrubby hill country of Texas. At various times he worked as a rancher, cotton trader, schoolteacher, real estate salesman, and railroad inspector. From 1905 to 1909 and again from 1917 to 1925, he was a member of the Texas House of Representatives. One of Lyndon's fondest childhood memories was occasionally being able to sit in the gallery of the state legislature and watch his father debate on the floor.

To provide better schooling for their children, Rebekah and Sam moved the family fourteen miles east to Johnson City when Lyndon was five. Johnson City (named for Lyndon's grandfather) was a town with about three hundred people.

During his school years, Lyndon did many household chores. He also earned spare money as a hired hand on nearby farms, a shoeshine boy in the local barber shop, a typesetter in the town newspaper office, and a trapper of animals whose skins he sold.

At school Lyndon towered above most of his classmates. He was six feet, three inches tall by the time he turned fifteen. But he showed little interest in sports and disliked most of the subjects he was studying, especially math.

Politics, on the other hand, fascinated the teenager. He was senior-class president and a member of the debate team that won the county title in his final year of high school. According to the class prophecy, the other students decided that he would become governor of Texas. But Lyndon had an even higher goal. He confided to a classmate, "Someday I'm going to be president of the United States."[2]

Lyndon's parents wanted him to go to college after he graduated from high school in 1924, but the fifteen-year-old boy said he was not ready to settle down and become a serious student. Instead, with five friends, he set out in a Model T Ford in search of adventure and high-paying jobs in California. They thought they would "go out there and make a lot of easy money," Lyndon said later.[3]

For many months he tried his hand at every kind of work he could find. He became a fruit picker, then a dishwasher, later an elevator operator, but all these jobs paid low wages. Disappointed and often hungry, he finally returned home.

In Johnson City, Lyndon got a job on a road crew, driving trucks and scooping up the dirt where roads were to be built. His mother, however, kept urging him to enter Southwest Texas State Teachers College in San Marcos, only about forty miles from Johnson City. After sixteen months of hard manual labor, he was finally ready to accept his mother's advice. "I'd just got through January on the road gang," Lyndon explained, "and it was cold weather, very cold. At that moment the prospect of going to school in the spring had some appeal to me. I said I'd do it."[4]

Lyndon hitchhiked to the San Marcos campus to begin his studies to become a teacher. In college he became a champion debater, worked on the school newspaper, and played an active role in campus politics. He worked his way through college as a trash collector, janitor, and finally, assistant secretary to the college president.

Still, he needed more money to complete his education. So Johnson took nine months off to teach English and other subjects to Mexican-American children in the small town of Cotulla, south of San Antonio. He grew very fond of his students and persuaded the parents of many poor children to take an active part in school affairs.

The parents told him that one thing they wanted was more recreational opportunities for their children. "So we organized a choir, a baseball team for the boys, and a volleyball team for the girls," Johnson wrote in his memoirs. "Those parents became actively involved in the life of the school, once they realized they had a voice in it."[5]

Johnson graduated from college in 1930 and began

teaching public speaking and debate in a Houston high school. Then something happened in 1931 that entirely changed the course of his career. Richard Kleberg, a Democrat who had just won a seat in the United States House of Representatives, invited Lyndon to become his secretary in Washington, D.C.

Excited to be in the world of politics, Johnson worked diligently at his new job. Soon he acquired a reputation as an expert on how Congress operated, and he became familiar with nearly every bill that the legislators were debating. He demonstrated such outstanding political talents that in 1933 his co-workers elected him speaker of the "Little Congress," an organization of congressional secretaries.

In 1934, Johnson was introduced to Claudia Alta "Lady Bird" Taylor, the daughter of a wealthy Texas rancher. (As a baby she had gotten her nickname when a nurse said she was as pretty as a ladybird.) The day after Johnson met Lady Bird he proposed marriage to her. The twenty-one-year-old woman, having just graduated from the University of Texas, was shocked by this sudden proposal and turned it down.

Lyndon, however, was persistent; he sent her a torrent of love letters. When Lady Bird sought her father's advice, he told her, "Some of the best deals are made in a hurry."[6] Finally she agreed to the marriage, and the wedding was held on November 17, 1934.

Over the years, the couple had two daughters, Lynda Bird and Luci Baines. Their names were carefully selected so that the parents and their children all had the initials LBJ. (In 1967, Lynda Bird married Marine Captain Charles S. Robb, who became governor of Virginia in 1981 and a United States senator in 1989.)

At the time that Lyndon and Lady Bird were married, the United States was in the midst of the Great Depression. In 1935, President Franklin D. Roosevelt established the National Youth Administration (NYA) and appointed Johnson director of the NYA in Texas. Under Johnson's leadership, the state NYA helped colleges provide part-time jobs for many needy students. The NYA also offered full-time employment in public works jobs, such as building schools and libraries, to thousands of other young Texans.

Lyndon was the youngest director of a state NYA; he also was considered one of the best. President Roosevelt praised his accomplishments, and First Lady Eleanor Roosevelt visited Texas to observe firsthand the successful work being done by that state's energetic, efficient NYA director.

In 1937, when the U.S. congressman in Johnson's district died, Lyndon decided to compete for the vacant seat against eight other candidates. At that time, many people were critical of Roosevelt's proposal to expand the number of justices on the Supreme Court in order to add new members who would support his New Deal measures. Because Lyndon needed some way to separate himself from the other candidates, he boldly pledged that he was "one hundred percent for Roosevelt."[7] His strategy succeeded, and at the age of twenty-eight Lyndon Johnson was elected to the U.S. House of Representatives.

Johnson was reelected to the House for five more terms, sometimes without opposition. He helped bring a number of public works to Texas, including a large dam, military bases, and federally supported electric power to the state's farmers. He also supported public housing to clean up city slums and was an active member of the Naval Affairs Committee.

When one of the senators from Texas died in 1941, Johnson entered the special election for the vacant office. He campaigned vigorously but lost to Governor W. Lee O'Daniel by only 1,311 votes out of nearly 600,000 cast.

Five months after the election, Japanese planes bombarded Pearl Harbor in Hawaii. Johnson became the first member of Congress to enter active duty in World War II. A lieutenant commander in the navy, he was stationed in the South Pacific. While he was flying in a B-26 bomber in June 1942, his plane was hit several times by Japanese aircraft, but it managed to limp back to its base on the island of New Guinea. A short time later he returned to Washington because President Roosevelt ordered all members of Congress serving in the armed forces to resume their legislative duties.

In 1948, Johnson again tried to win a Senate seat. He staged a whirlwind campaign, traveling from one rally to another in a helicopter—a type of aircraft that few Texas ranchers and farmers had ever seen. Since the votes in the Democratic primary were divided among eleven candidates and none won a majority, a run-off election was held between the two Democrats with the most votes. They were Lyndon Johnson and Coke Stevenson, a popular former governor.

The election was extremely close. After bitter court battles about the results, Johnson was declared the winner by only eighty-seven votes out of nearly one million votes cast. In the 1940s, the Republican Party in Texas was very small and weak, so Johnson had no trouble defeating his Republican rival in the general election.

Senator Johnson began to win national attention as chairman of the Preparedness Investigating Subcommittee. Its investigations saved the nation more than $5 billion by exposure of wasteful practices and inefficiency during the Korean War. An early supporter of the nation's space program, LBJ was the first chairman of the Senate Aeronautics and Space Sciences Committee.

More than any other senator in recent history, Johnson practiced the art of wheeling and dealing in order to get Congress to pass the bills he supported. One observer said that this senator from Texas served up "an incredibly potent mixture of persuasion, badgering, flattery, threats, reminders of past favors, and future advantages [favors]."[8]

Johnson's strong powers of persuasion were recognized by the other Democratic senators. In 1951, they named him the party "whip" who was responsible for prodding his Democratic colleagues to follow the party's philosophy and to be in attendance whenever the Senate voted. Two years later, he was elected minority leader of the Senate. At that time, Dwight D. Eisenhower was president and the Republicans held a majority of seats in Congress.

In 1954, LBJ easily won reelection, and in that year's congressional elections the Democrats gained enough seats to take control of both the Senate and the House. At the age of forty-six, Johnson became the youngest majority leader in the Senate's history.

Even though Republican Eisenhower was president and the Democrats controlled Congress, Johnson was determined that whenever possible, Congress should work with instead of against the president. This philosophy of cooperation was based on a saying from the prophet Isaiah that LBJ often quoted, "Come now, let us reason together."⁹ Through conciliation and compromise between the legislators and the president, many important bills were enacted into law.

Johnson did not actively campaign in the 1960 race for the Democratic nomination for the presidency. Nevertheless, at the Democratic National Convention he had more delegates' votes than any other candidate except the winner, John F. Kennedy. Because the majority leader of the Senate plays a much larger role in government business than the vice president, many political experts were surprised when Johnson accepted Kennedy's offer to be his running mate. But if LBJ had not been on the ticket to help the Democrats carry several southern and southwestern states, it is doubtful that Kennedy would have been elected president in this very close election.

Johnson continued to work hard as vice president. He served as the chairman of the National Aeronautics and Space Council, the President's Committee on Equal Employment Opportunities, and the Peace Corps Advisory Council. Also, he traveled throughout the world as the president's goodwill ambassador.

Vice President and Mrs. Johnson were riding two cars behind the president's car in the Dallas motorcade on the fateful day when Kennedy was assassinated. As soon as he learned that the president was dead, Johnson rushed to the Dallas airport to return to Washington. Aboard *Air Force One* he took the oath of office that was administered by Sarah T. Hughes, a federal judge.

Johnson later recalled that in the shock and confusion following the tragic event, "People were grievin' and cryin' and hidin' their babies under the bed. It wasn't my choice," he said, "but I was the only President they had. I did the best I knew how."[10]

In a nationally televised address to Congress a few days after Kennedy's funeral, Johnson urged the lawmakers to honor the slain president's memory by finally passing Kennedy's major civil rights bill that had stalled in Congress. "We have talked long enough in this country about equal rights," the new president declared. "It is time now to write the next chapter—and to write it into the books of law."[11]

Congress responded by passing the landmark Civil Rights Act of 1964. It was the most sweeping civil rights legislation in the nation's history and provided, among other things, equal access for African-Americans to all places of "public accommodation," such as restaurants, hotels, theaters, ballparks, and restrooms.

The following year, President Johnson signed the Voting Rights Law. It banned literacy tests for voters and ordered the federal government to send voting registrars to any district where half or more of the adult population was not registered to vote. This law provided a large increase of black voters in many southern states. Another major civil rights act during Johnson's presidency forbade discrimination in the sale and rental of houses and apartments.

In 1964, President Johnson proposed a bold program of reforms that he felt would bring to all Americans the benefits of a "Great Society." "In our time," he declared, "we have the opportunity to move not only toward the rich society and the powerful society, but upward to the Great Society. The Great Society rests on abundance and liberty for all. It demands an end to poverty and racial injustices."[12]

The presidential election of 1964 occurred before Congress could act on most parts of the Great Society program. Johnson's opponent was a very conservative Republican, Senator Barry M. Goldwater of Arizona. When the votes were counted, Johnson had won reelection by one of the largest landslides in American history, receiving 61.1 percent of the popular vote. Capturing all but six states, LBJ gained 486 electoral votes to Goldwater's 52. Senator Hubert H. Humphrey of Minnesota, Johnson's running mate, became vice president.

Interpreting his huge election victory as a signal to press forward with his Great Society proposals, President Johnson convinced Congress to enact many new laws. One important measure was Medicare, which provided medical benefits to people sixty-five years of age or older. It was financed by an increase in the Social Security tax. Another measure was federal aid to Appalachia, a poverty-stricken region in the eastern part of the United States. Large federal grants were given to every level of education, ranging from Head Start for preschoolers through scholarships, loans, and part-time jobs for college students. VISTA was established as a Peace Corps operating in the United States. Child day-care facilities were started, so that mothers in poor families could be freed to work.

Protecting the environment was another important phase of the Great Society program. Congress passed the first significant acts designed to provide clean air and water. Lady Bird Johnson played a large role in promoting citizen support for improving the appearance of highways. She pressured Congress to pass the Highway Beautification Act (nicknamed the "Lady Bird Bill"), which required the removal of many billboards and other signs on sections of major highways.

Critics of the Great Society program charged that it was costing too much money and putting the national government much further into debt. And they argued that the president's war on poverty was not succeeding in improving the living standards of large numbers of poor people.

The president's popularity, however, did not decline sharply until he greatly increased the role of the United States in the Vietnam War. To preserve its independence, non-Communist South Vietnam had been fighting for several years against two allied foes: aggressors from Communist North Vietnam and Communist guerrilla forces inside South Vietnam, who were called the Vietcong.

The United States had helped South Korea and other non-Communist countries repel Communist invaders. It strongly opposed a Communist takeover of South Vietnam. But American presidents before Johnson had hesitated to become deeply involved in a conflict in faraway Southeast Asia fought between different groups of Vietnamese people. President Eisenhower had sent financial aid and less than a thousand military advisers to South Vietnam. While Kennedy was in the White House, about sixteen thousand American military advisers were stationed in South Vietnam, but they were limited to noncombat duties.

President Johnson, however, was so determined that South Vietnam must not fall to the Communists that he changed the role of the Americans stationed there from military advisers to combat troops. He firmly believed that the military might of the United States could subdue the small country of North Vietnam. Beginning in 1965, the size of the U.S. forces in the Vietnam War increased sharply every year. By 1968 more than half a million Americans were fighting in this Asian conflict.

At home, the Vietnam War led to angry demonstrations and vicious charges that President Johnson was a murderer because he had permitted thousands of Americans to be killed in a futile war that did not endanger the security of the United States. Antiwar protesters cried out against the tragic war on college campuses, in bloody street riots, and finally in the halls of Congress, where many lawmakers demanded that American forces be pulled out of Vietnam.

Discouraged, disillusioned, and in failing health, President Johnson grimly announced in 1968 that he would not seek another term in the White House. He retired to his LBJ Ranch in Texas.

The war dragged on, and the last American troops were not sent home until 1973, during the second presidential term of Richard Nixon. By this time, U.S. planes had dropped more bombs on North Vietnam than they had dropped on all enemy targets during World War II. Two years later, the victorious North Vietnamese completed the conquest of South Vietnam and added its land to their country. More than fifty-seven thousand Americans died in the only war the United States ever lost.

Johnson died at his ranch in Texas on January 22, 1973. Looking back on his presidential administration, Lyndon Johnson fully understood both the powers and the limitations of the person who holds the highest office in the land. "The presidency," he said, "has made every man who occupied it, no matter how small, bigger than he was, and no matter how big, not big enough for its demands."[13]

SOURCE NOTES

1

1. Stephen E. Ambrose, *Eisenhower: Soldier and President* (New York: Simon and Schuster, 1990), 15–16.

2. Stephen E. Ambrose, *Ike: Abilene to Berlin* (New York: Harper and Row, 1973), 19.

3. Edmund Lindop and Joseph Jares, *White House Sportsmen* (Boston: Houghton Mifflin, 1964), 15.

4. Ibid., 19.

5. Dwight D. Eisenhower, *At Ease: Stories I Tell to Friends* (Garden City, N.Y.: Doubleday, 1967), 113.

6. Jim Hargrove, *Dwight D. Eisenhower* (Chicago: Childrens Press, 1987), 52.

7. *Newsweek*, May 23, 1994, 20.

8. "O.K. Let's Go!" *American History Magazine*, June 1994, 39.

9. Hargrove, *Dwight D. Eisenhower*, 53.

10. Elizabeth Van Steenwyk, *Dwight D. Eisenhower, President* (New York: Walker, 1987), 99.

11. Walter Lafeber, *The American Age: United States Foreign Policy at Home and Abroad Since 1750* (New York: Norton, 1989), 544.

12. *New York Times*, March 29, 1969, 22.

2

1. Edmund Lindop and Joseph Jares, *White House Sportsmen*, 129.

2. Zachary Kent, *John F. Kennedy* (Chicago: Childrens Press, 1987), 18.

3. Catherine Corley Anderson, *John F. Kennedy: Young People's President* (Minneapolis: Lerner, 1991), 29.

4. Barbara Harrison and David Terris, *A Twilight Struggle: The Life of John Fitzgerald Kennedy* (New York: Lothrop, Lee and Shepard, 1992), 26.

5. William Manchester, *One Bright Shining Moment: Remembering Kennedy* (Boston: Little, Brown, 1983), 10.

6. Kenneth O'Donnell and David F. Powers, *Johnny, We Hardly Knew Ye: Memories of John Fitzgerald Kennedy* (Boston: Little, Brown, 1972), 113.

7. Theodore C. Sorensen, ed., *Let the Word Go Forth: The Speeches, Statements, and Writings of John F. Kennedy, 1947 to 1963* (New York: Delacorte, 1988), 131.

8. Michael Barone, *Our Country: The Shaping of America From Roosevelt to Reagan* (New York: Free Press, 1990), 336.

9. *U.S. News & World Report*, July 11, 1994, 51.

10. Richard Reeves, *President Kennedy: Profile of Power* (New York: Simon and Schuster, 1993), 138.

11. Ibid., 154.

12. Sorensen, *Let the Word Go Forth*, 327–328.

13. I. E. Levine, *John Kennedy: Young Man in the White House* (Lakeville, Conn.: Grey Castle Press, 1991), 161–162.

14. William Manchester, *The Death of a President* (New York: Harper/Perennial, 1988), 153.

3

1. Dudley Lynch, *The President from Texas: Lyndon Baines Johnson* (New York: Crowell, 1975), 3.

2. Alfred Steinberg, *Sam Johnson's Boy: A Close-up of the President from Texas* (New York: Macmillan, 1968), 30.

3. Robert Dallek, *Lone Star Rising: Lyndon Johnson and His Times*, 1908–1960 (New York: Oxford University Press, 1991), 58.

4. Merle Miller, *Lyndon: An Oral Biography* (New York: Putnam, 1980), 26–27.

5. Lyndon Baines Johnson, *The Vantage Point: Perspectives of the Presidency, 1963–1969* (New York: Holt, Rinehart and Winston, 1971), 75.

6. Arden Davis Melick, *Wives of the Presidents* (Maplewood, N.J.: Hammond, 1985), 82.

7. Robert A. Caro, *The Years of Lyndon Johnson: The Path to Power* (New York: Knopf, 1982), 404.

8. Jim Hargrove, *Lyndon B. Johnson* (Chicago: Childrens Press, 1987), 54.

9. Lynch, *The President from Texas*, 74.

10. Hugh Sidey, "Reach Out and Twist an Arm," *Time*, December 13, 1993, 43.

11. "Address Before a Joint Session of Congress," November 27, 1963, *Public Papers of the Presidents: Lyndon Baines Johnson* (Washington, D.C.: Government Printing Office, 1966), 9.

12. "Remarks at the University of Michigan, Ann Arbor," May 22, 1964, *Public Papers of the Presidents: Lyndon Baines Johnson* (Washington, D.C.: Government Printing Office, 1966), 704.

13. *U.S. News & World Report*, May 30, 1994, 11.

FURTHER READING

Ambrose, Stephen E. *Ike: Abilene to Berlin.* New York: Harper and Row, 1973.

Anderson, Catherine Corley. *John F. Kennedy: Young People's President.* Minneapolis: Lerner, 1991.

Beard, Charles A. *Charles A. Beard's the Presidents in American History.* Rev. ed. Englewood Cliffs, N.J.: Messner, 1989.

Becker, Elizabeth. *America's Vietnam War: A Narrative History.* Boston: Houghton Mifflin, 1992.

Blassingame, Wyatt. *The Look-It-Up Book of Presidents.* Rev. ed. New York: Random House, 1992.

Blodgett, Bonnie, and J. T. Tice. *At Home With the Presidents.* Woodstock, N.Y.: Overlook Press, 1988.

Blumberg, Rhoda. *First Ladies.* New York: Franklin Watts, 1981.

Cannon, Marian G. *Dwight David Eisenhower.* New York: Franklin Watts, 1990.

Clinton, Susan. *The Cuban Missile Crisis.* Chicago: Childrens Press, 1993.

Coy, Harold. *The First Book of Presidents.* Rev. ed. New York: Franklin Watts, 1985.

Darby, Jean. *Dwight D. Eisenhower: A Man Called Ike.* Minneapolis: Lerner, 1989.

Denenberg, Barry. *John Fitzgerald Kennedy: America's 35th President.* New York: Scholastic, 1988.

Eskow, Dennis. *Lyndon Baines Johnson.* New York: Franklin Watts, 1993.

Faber, Doris. *Dwight Eisenhower.* New York: Abelard-Schuman, 1977.

Garrison, Webb. *A Treasury of White House Tales.* Nashville: Rutledge Hills Press, 1989.

Hargrove, Jim. *Dwight D. Eisenhower.* Chicago: Childrens Press, 1987.

————. *Lyndon B. Johnson.* Chicago: Childrens Press, 1987.

Harrison, Barbara, and Daniel Terris. *A Twilight Struggle: The Life of John Fitzgerald Kennedy.* New York: Lothrop, Lee and Shepard, 1992.

Hoobler, Dorothy, and Thomas Hoobler. *Vietnam: Why We Fought.* New York: Knopf, 1990.

Kelly, C. Brian. *Best Little Stories From the White House.* Charlottesville, Va.: Montpelier Publishing, 1992.

Kent, Zachary. *John F. Kennedy.* Chicago: Childrens Press, 1987.

Lawson, Don. *The United States in the Vietnam War.* New York: HarperCollins, 1981.

Levine, I. E. *John Kennedy: Young Man in the White House.* Lakeville, Conn.: Grey Castle Press, 1991.

Lindop, Edmund, and Joseph Jares. *White House Sportsmen.* Boston: Houghton Mifflin, 1964.

Lynch, Dudley. *The President from Texas: Lyndon Baines Johnson.* New York: Crowell, 1975.

Melick, Arden Davis. *Wives of the Presidents.* Maplewood, N.J.: Hammond, 1985.

Mills, Judie. *John F. Kennedy.* New York: Franklin Watts, 1988.

Pious, Richard. *The Presidency.* Columbus, Ohio: Silver Burdett, 1991.

Randall, Marta. *John F. Kennedy.* New York: Chelsea House, 1988.

Selfridge, John W. *John F. Kennedy: Courage in Crisis.* New York: Fawcett Columbine, 1989.

Stein, R. Conrad. *The Assassination of John F. Kennedy.* Chicago: Childrens Press, 1992.

Stein, R. Conrad. *D-Day.* Chicago: Childrens Press, 1993.

———. *The Powers of the President.* Chicago: Childrens Press, 1985.

Van Steenwyck, Elizabeth. *Dwight D. Eisenhower, President.* New York: Walker, 1987.

OTHER SOURCES OF INFORMATION

Alistair Cooke's America: The Arsenal (World War II). Videocassette. Grades 5 and up. BBC/TimeLife Video. Filmic Archives, the Cinema Center, Botsford, CT 06404.

Basic American History, Program 2: Post–Civil War to the Present. Computer disks for both IBM and Apple. Grades 7 and up. Social Studies School Service, 10200 Jefferson Blvd., P.O. Box 802, Culver City, CA 90232.

Before Gorbachev: From Stalin to Brezhnev. Videocassette. Grades 7 and up. Filmic Archives, the Cinema Center, Botsford, CT 06404.

The Civil Rights Movement: Witness to History. Videocassette. Grades 5 and up. Guidance Associates, P.O. Box 3000, Mt. Kisco, NY 10549.

Cuban Missile Crisis. Videocassette. Grades 5 and up. WGBH Boston. Hearst Entertainment, 235 E. 45th St., New York, NY 10017.

D-Day Remembered. Film. Grades 5 and up. National D-Day Museum. The Video Catalog, P.O. Box 64267, St. Paul, MN 55164.

The Eagle and the Bear: U.S.-Soviet Relations Since World War II. Videocassette or 4 filmstrips/4 audiocassettes. Grades 7 and up. Guidance Associates, P.O. Box 3000, Mt. Kisco, NY 10549.

Eisenhower. Videocassette. Grades 5 and up. CBS. Ambrose Video Publishing, 1290 Avenue of the Americas, Ste. 2245, New York, NY 10104.

Eisenhower: The Contentious Years. Two videocassettes. Grades 7 and up. Churchill Media, P.O. Box 251233, Los Angeles, CA 90025.

Eisenhower: The Dangerous Years. Two videocassettes. Grades 7 and up. Churchill Media, P.O. Box 251233, Los Angeles, CA 90025.

The Great Debates: John F. Kennedy vs. Richard M. Nixon. Videocassette. Grades 7 and up. Filmic Archives, the Cinema Center, Botsford, CT 06404.

The Iron Curtain. Videocassette. Grades 5 and up. Britannica Learning Materials, 310 South Michigan Ave., Chicago, IL 60604.

JFK and the Cuban Missile Crisis. Simulations. Grades 7 and up. Interact. Social Studies School Service, 10200 Jefferson Blvd., P.O. Box 802, Culver City, CA 90232.

JFK Assassination. CD-ROM for IBM and Macintosh. Grades 7 and up. The Video Catalog, P.O. Box 64267, St. Paul, MN 55164.

JFK Remembered. Videocassette. Grades 5 and up. ABC. Filmic Archives, the Cinema Center, Botsford, CT 06404.

John Fitzgerald Kennedy: A Celebration of His Life and Times. Laser disc. Grades 7 and up. Filmic Archives, the Cinema Center, Botsford, CT 06404.

The Johnson Years. Videocassette. Grades 7 and up. UPI Television News. Journal Films, 1560 Sherman Ave., Ste. 100, Evanston, IL 60201.

The Kennedys, 1900–1980. Two videocassettes. Grades 5 and up. PBS. Cambridge Educational, Box 2153, Charleston, WV 25328.

The Korean War. Five videocassettes. Grades 5 and up. Korean Broadcast System. The Video Catalog, P.O. Box 64267, St. Paul, MN 55164.

Korea: The Forgotten War. Videocassette. Grades 5 and up. Filmic Archives, the Cinema Center, Botsford, CT 06404.

LBJ: A Biography. Two videocassettes. Grades 7 and up. PBS. Pacific Arts Video, 11858 La Grange Ave., Los Angeles, CA 90025.

LBJ: The Early Years. Videocassette. Grades 5 and up. Fries Entertainment. Fries Home Video, 6922 Hollywood Blvd., 12th floor, Hollywood, CA 90028.

Living American History Series: U.S. History IV (1915–1960). Primary source materials for Apple or IBM computers. Grades 7 and up. Priven Learning Systems. Social Studies School Service, 10200 Jefferson Blvd., P.O. Box 802, Culver City, CA 90232.

Lyndon B. Johnson. Videocassette. Grades 7 and up. WGBH Boston. Hearst Entertainment, 235 E. 45th St., New York, NY 10017.

Martin, the Emancipator (Martin Luther King Jr.). Videocassette. Grades 5 and up. Social Studies School Service, 10200 Jefferson Blvd., P.O. Box 802, Culver City, CA 90232.

Milestone Documents: The Cuban Missile Crisis. Facsimile of primary source materials. Grades 6 and up. National Archives. Education Branch, NARA, Washington, DC 20408

Milestone Documents: Kennedy's Inaugural Address. Facsimile of primary source materials. Grades 6 and up. National Archives. Education Branch, NARA, Washington, DC 20408.

Modern America: The Primary Source, Volume 4. Photocopy masters of primary sources. Grades 7 and up. Perfection Form. Social Studies School Service, 10200 Jefferson Blvd., P.O. Box 802, Culver City, CA 90232.

Normandy: The Great Crusade. CD-ROM for IBM. Grades 5 and up. The Video Catalog, P.O. Box 64267, St. Paul, MN 55164.

The Presidents. Videocassette. Grades 7 and up. Post Newsweek Section. Lucerne Media, 37 Ground Pine Road, Morris Plains, NJ 07950.

The Presidents: It All Started with George. CD-ROM for IBM. Grades 5 and up. National Geographic/IBM. National Geographic Educational Services, P.O. Box 98019, Washington, DC 20090.

U.S. History on CD-ROM. CD-ROM for both IBM and Macintosh. Grades 7 and up. Bureau Development, Inc. Social Studies School Service, 10200 Jefferson Blvd., P.O. Box 802, Culver City, CA 90232.

Vietnam: Chronicle of a War. Videocassette. Grades 7 and up. CBS News. CBS/Fox Video, 1330 Avenue of the Americas, 5th floor, New York, NY 10019.

Vietnam Experience. Videocassette. Grades 5 and up. Filmic Archives, the Cinema Center, Botsford, CT 06404.

Vietnam: The War at Home. Videocassette. Grades 5 and up. Filmic Archives, the Cinema Center, Botsford, CT 06404.

World War II: North Africa to Germany. Film. Grades 7 and up. BFA Educational Media, 468 Park Avenue South, New York, NY 10016.